Runic

David Appelbaum

ISBN: 978-93-6354-477-2

First Edition: 2026
Rs. 200/-

Cyberwit.net
HIG 45 Kaushambi Kunj, Kalindipuram
Allahabad - 211011 (U.P.) India
http://www.cyberwit.net
Tel: +(91) 9415091004
E-mail: info@cyberwit.net

Printed at Repro India Limited.

1.
Shaft of sun
weaves spiders' threads

me inside
on a private matter

table talk
competes with:

a nearby interstate.

The way commerce
follows the iron rail

mapping curlicues
on a dollar sign.

I'm touching on
a subject as moot

as gender reveal.

Baby spiders cascade
like isotopes

upwardly faring
nether shadows

streaming their dark
plateau of obsession.

2.
Secrets invite
murmurs

let me make
(the artiste)

my paradise
of numinous folds.

We lip-synced a future
undoing since

sign language
just repeats

what hasn't yet occurred
leaving memory out—

grace is heeding.

. . .

The only reason
for pessimism

is anyone's eyes
when cupped

look sad.

3.
Wave particle interaction
has me in a tizzy.

Was it a heated relation
stolen moments

bus ticket stubs?

In reality, nothing
vibrates

there are control freaks
who say there's no

God-particle

reality is mundane
just traces of dust

bracketing what waits
for what proceeds,

it's dual
too complex to follow

the news coming out.
self-annihilates

Hallelujah!

4.
'Warm the cockles
of her heart. . .'

It's hard to have
good ideas

while reading road signs
that clutter her lawn.

. . . .

Does it mean
she's closed

a shell
clammed up

allowing just another
trickle

of what's suddenly
ingested?

. . . .

One can find oneself
hypnotized

by nothing
while farther down

the tender inside
of feeling

with no cold neuron
tics

no longer shuns
its all-forgiving task,

unpenting the breath..

5.
Ready to turn the page
this chapter's over?

Few are willing
to risk paper cuts

in recent novels
how many heroines
use seductive power's
snake-like venom?

Clothed in sunlit scoops
young innocence

suited coveralls
and patchwork cloaks

whose tattings talk
around weak plots

trying to earn
some denouement.

before action
can be flipped

inverting the motive.
Murder hornets

skirmish with
tea roses.

under clouds of
pesticide.

6.
Time travel
is like dividing

the sea, tossed
twinkling

aside, before it returns.
You end up back

where you know
you were holding

an option
to be present,

feeling to appear
in human form

is by birth a right.

Circles of light
on the porch hosta

wink, held by
ropes aloft

when you dream
does it feel like

meeting someone
you once knew?

7.
Elbow in line,
it wasn't her fault

she couldn't explain
the need

to fluff lacy
ruffles

like a pin cushion
prickly but stout

and had to be first.

Jonquils also race
the sun themselves

before second frost

loving themselves like she
when she felt

a girl in her
coiled up

now unbend, passing
the way through

the front door

no secret at all

8.
Little crystalline seed
opens horizons

take a step back
for an acrobatic look

between your legs.
For centuries, science

has tried to explain
it's better

when enthusiasms
have motives

that would return you
to their roots

or does it only work
autonomously

like dances
in Poland

when you're born
to the kazatsky,

the moon looks bigger.

9.
Genealogy 101 is
sly as a fox

lineages have hedges
where gaps

are precluded
by your analyst,

where does she fit?

Knuckle over swollen
knuckle, getting down

to brass tacks,
using a counter

to trace radioactivity.

No, he said 'destiny'

as if on a long trek
through the Mid-west

where foxy is for
cheap epigenetics.

10.
Teleprompting is
one way to stay ahead

of the game
but because cellphone towers

glass and plastic
disguised as trees

cause unconscious flares
of aphasia

you have to swallow
ends of sentences.

We're becoming
like Brits, clipped

and sped straight
letter by letter

to the speakers' acquired
habit of lisping.

Do you ever try
lip sync?

11.
Black holes salute
negation
they weren't anywhere before

non-attachment
is like that,
a Midas touch reversed.

Haloes get crowned
by their surrounds

occasionally reaping
pre-existence

rung by rung
in explosive decay.

Feeling haunts us
the same way
behind a smile

to materialize in tears
'sorrow to excess . . .'

we are said
to orbit that point
that lights the dark

who is there
to tell us when
to jump?

12,
Bellyaching frogs
alarmed by cold

reject the given
object, pity,

yellow slime
around the well.

No map in memory
of overnight

migration

but a boy
grabbing pollywogs of

the two sorts—
we'll never know

what matters next,
captivity of

Laissez faire!

13.
leaf figures look
real

one tames a lion

taming is shameful
safari haters say

it mocks fierceness
of the beast.

Biblical dominion
gives a passport

to human mastery

cut up nature
and it's art you get

look again
it seems a teakettle

soothingly homespun.

Please pass me
the scissors

14.
A dancing bear
is one example

does a word exist for it?

When thinking
philosophizes disgrace

don't make
a constellation
of pinpricks

or a magnifier
from a gold drop

hung on a starflower

entrepreneurial crows
mingle below

winter trees
at dusk

caws follow
their investment method

of counting

15.
Neutrino fog
happens when you dicker
small minds

take a step back
big ideas are
hard to come by

like how to avoid
emotional
inheritance

. . . .

this tells more
than you believe you know

like an intention
that's apter

inside brawn and guts

before syntax
lists contrary hopes

anyone can be mesmerized

in street play
one penny monty

. . . .

you should disrespect
what's said to you

when it comes
over and again.

like deja vu

16.
TGIF
When did it come
to bullying?

If prayers
are tufted
in acronyms

like wildcat
ears

it's because
morning stillness
with its qualms

pangs itches
shivers

unprovoked
discontinuities

lacks reality
like when wheezing

haunts one room
and vanishes in the next.

and it's a robovac

17.
the peak is a slit
that lights

a rupestral slope
to ground zero.

Instead of
what is to be said

I have an impulse
to skip the whole thing

why did I agree
to the rock conference

speakers slide down a
steel chute

tough on the jeans
power down

kick the screen
and it runs

blue in dark blue
pixels

the unconscious
can't see

gradients.

18.
Black Friday
sobs *mammon*

when did it lose
spunk?

It partakes
of the future

when added quality
costs

all sales final

since wealth
owns the top

a distant goal
for fourth graders

they already know dress
counts

in being liked
as does cash

when you
are rich

no one cares
how you look.

19.
The short end
of the stick

means there's a
longer end

choosing is counted
a job skill

discerning is never
a measure

of indifference
but a bet

on half-formed
letters to pick

a would be
letting chance

seek the thrill

of actuality.

I'll do anything
for attention

20.
'emergency pry bar'
is only a picture

between windows
of the 3:48 to Croton

catching occasional
bursts of sun

like a lunatic's
idea of rage

. . . .

a rock thrown
at the moving car

has a curve
like a parabola

and seemed to step back
upon missing

but with an echo
to remind us

of near collisions
yet to happen.

21.
dappling gray
pale moonlight

what does it mean
when a word
pops into your brain?

there's a hollow
we must suppose

reality yet to shroud

a deeper zone
that repeats
like a bullfrog

you almost recognize
except the floor

is darkened
scattered baby toys
lying in wait

'Better do it now,'
courage says

one must wake
repeat a talisman:
sun in your lap

'Not a bad day'

22.
'A teakettle for Eleanor'
why do we look
for new things

when a long life
with happy children
will do?

Imagine a person
just like you

perfectly transparent
perfectly opaque

no ambitions
can one trait disgrace another?

Functional babble
doesn't equal faith
you'll be ready

the first innovation
will be serial
scare quotes

a citation
which is a kind
of stop

when a personality

runs out of
trash to mouth

start over: it's
like swallowing

a splinter

23.
Black Friday deals
include oven air fryers

to be conscious is to go
through moments

typically assigned to
choice of kitchen gadgets

scraper or ladle

angular motion invites
a spiral down

center of which is
farthest away

light raw rampant
point to imagined point

winking from
the shady corner bouquet

minus tomorrow's sale

you never know what
offer will be next

bring scissors.
for coupons

24.
a wake is
a vee

yes, she said
what story follows
where it's headed?

Asleep,
we're negligently vigilant

scrolling pages
for a passkey

where does the brace fit in?

rippled at edges
lapping playfully
on one cloudy shoal

lolling along on
a long discovery voyage
through a disaster

that takes place
in the plot

carpe diem

25.
there are things
to do
for instance, jettison

all ideals
or like, continue

hurtling
down the ramparts

to smell the witch
hazel
fresh from first frost

continuity
is to start over
escape iteration

its new invention
is repetition
do it once

and forget about it

is that for real?

An attention
so empty

it’s parody

of what
the riddle is

26.
sulfur storms
on Mars

heavens!
Who'd have expected

interplanetary hell?
check the box

if you believe
masculinity

is to blame

I admit I confuse
signs with messages

and do it
with no malice

as if I'm at times
a photometer

daylight fades
the evening star

appears
Venus is blue

27.
is it spam
'The truth will come'?

a gnawing hunger
then actual
gnawing

people react
as if role-models
weren't camo . . .

. . . .

to feel fab
after these dreams

distopic
yet a sweet thrill
at first

yes, we did
ask to be born

but under
the breath

a poem exists
to mark it

this one
is a way

to talk to
the other possibility,

that I'm wrong

28.
temporal grammar
is miles off
it’s a syntax of

pings
(as in déjà vu)

cold memory
seems fixed

barely abreast
of things

now yesterday’s
baby mice

are cavorting
beneath

our barberry bush
in its funerary

phase

all thorns.

29.
strategic navigation
that polyps indulge

chancy ocean currents
creatures
that never wake

can sprout a whole new
reef

with one single wave of sperm
this may be wrong

shall we talk
about sex

gloating for centuries?

to make
out of nothing

those steely gleams
or sensational chills

is a project
that can end on a reef

know any good counselors?

30.
'I need a pair of tweezers.'
Is that one or two?

No question could be
more bizarre

our numbering is
a parody
of human intellect

sprawled
over the earth

to fake it is to imagine
otherwise

the same confusion
surrounds our
animal origin

of course any thought
about our 'progenitor'
is a shot
in the dark

this poem exists
to repurpose it.

best to get a grip
and pinch hard.

31.
Dark matter is
evolving

I just want
to understand

waves, waves
stretched to obscurity

or into the light?

It calms me
to watch

treetops
disappear

without excuse

into the almost
visible night

www.ingramcontent.com/pod-product-compliance
Ingram Content Group UK Ltd.
Pitfield, Milton Keynes, MK11 3LW, UK
UKHW041316190726
13845UKWH00025B/320

9 789363 544772